D0504482

Bee

Karen Hartley
and
Chris Macro

First published in Great Britain by Heinemann Library
Halley Court, Jordan Hill, Oxford OX2 8EJ
a division of Reed Educational and Professional Publishing Ltd.
Heinemann is a registered trademark of Reed Educational & Professional Publishing Limited.

OXFORD FLORENCE PRAGUE MADRID ATHENS
MELBOURNE AUCKLAND KUALA LUMPUR SINGAPORE TOKYO
IBADAN NAIROBI KAMPALA JOHANNESBURG GABORONE
PORTSMOUTH NH CHICAGO MEXICO CITY SAO PAULO

Designed by Celia Floyd
Illustrations by Alan Male
Printed in Hong Kong / China

02 01 00 99 98
10 9 8 7 6 5 4 3 2 1

ISBN 0 431 01673 9

British Library Cataloguing in Publication Data

Hartley, Karen
Bee. - (Bug books)
1.Bee - Juvenile literature
I.Title II.Macro, Chris
595.7'99

Acknowledgements
The Publishers would like to thank the following for permission to reproduce photographs:
Bruce Coleman Ltd: J Brackenbury p10, J Cancalosi p11, J Shaw p21, K Taylor pp8, 12; NHPA: N Callow p28, S Dalton pp4, 13, 16, 17, 18, 19, 20, 26; Oxford Scientific Films: G Bernard pp22, 29, S Camazine p15, G Dew p24, B Osborne p7, R Packwood p6, D Thompson pp5, 9, 14, 23, 27; Premaphotos: K Preston-Mafham p25

Cover photograph reproduced with permission of child: Chris Honeywell; bee: D Maitland/Telegraph Colour Library

Every effort has been made to contact copyright holders of any material reproduced in this book. Any omissions will be rectified in subsequent printings if notice is given to the Publisher.

Any words appearing in the text in bold, **like this**, are explained in the Glossary.

Contents

What are bees?

Bees are furry **insects** with six legs and two pairs of **transparent** wings. They flap their wings so quickly that they make a buzzing sound as they fly.

There are different kinds of bees and each kind has queens, **drones** and worker bees. Some bees live together in nests but some live by themselves.

Where do bees live?

Bumblebees live together in a nest in long grass or underground. Bees choose to live in places where flowers grow, like parks and gardens.

Honeybees live together in a nest in a **hollow** tree or log. Sometimes people keep honeybees in a wooden hive. We are going to look at some honeybees.

What do bees look like?

Bees have hairs that are different colours on their bodies. They make the bee's stripes look brown and yellow.

All bees have two large eyes which can see up, down, backwards and forwards at the same time. They also have three small eyes. They have two **feelers** for touching and smelling.

How big are bees?

Bumblebees, like this one, are about the size of a grape. Honeybees are about the size of a peanut. Sometimes their tongues are not long enough to reach the **nectar** in big flowers.

Queen bees are always bigger than worker bees and **drones**. Worker bees are always the smallest kind in the nest. There is only one queen in each nest.

How are bees born?

In the spring the queen bee **mates** with a **drone**. She then lays her eggs in special places called cells, inside the nest.

After 3 days the **larvae hatch** from the eggs. They are small and white. They have no eyes, no legs and no wings. They are fed by the worker bees.

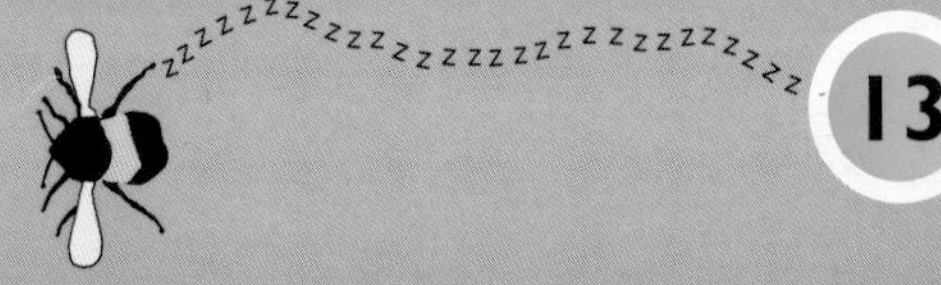

How do honeybees grow?

After 5 days the **larvae** turn into **pupae** and begin to turn into adult bees. After 2 weeks the new bees push off the tops of the cells and crawl out.

The bees' bodies are very soft but they soon get harder. Most of the new bees are worker bees and at first they work inside the nest.

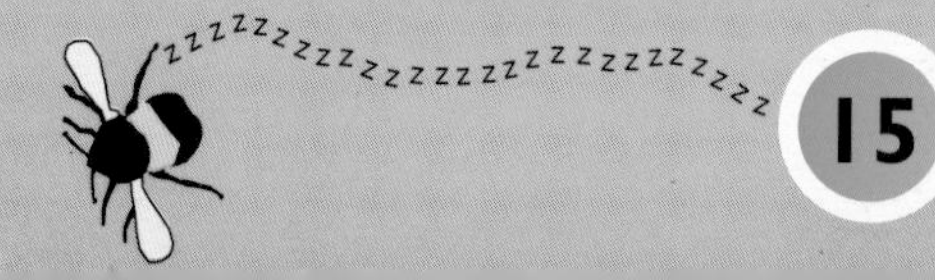

What do bees eat?

Bees eat the **pollen** from flowers. They bring **nectar** from the flowers to the nest to make into honey. They eat the honey in cold weather.

When the **larvae** are in the cells they need to eat to grow. Worker bees feed them on honey and pollen.

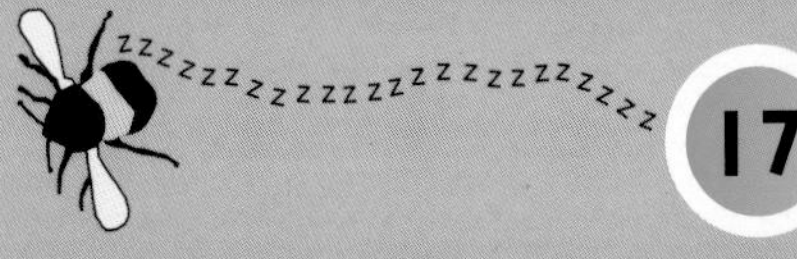

Which animals attack bees?

Queens and worker bees will **sting** if they are frightened or angry. Their stripes give a warning to other insects not to come near them. Some birds, like the one in the picture, eat bees.

Some worker bees stand at the entrance to the nest to guard it. They will fight bees from other nests if they have come to steal honey.

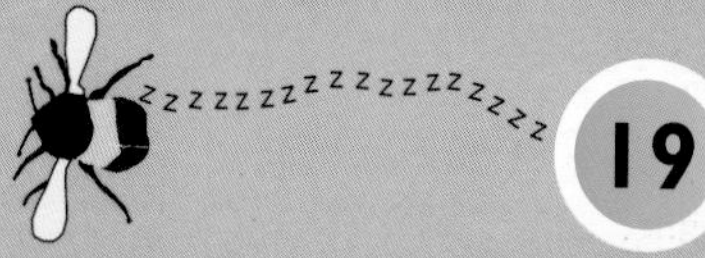

How do honeybees move?

All bees have strong wings so they can fly a long way to look for food. When it is hot they fan their wings to keep the nest cool.

When bees land on a flower they crawl inside it to suck up the **nectar** and collect **pollen**. They wave their **feelers** to help them smell and taste.

zzzzzzzzzzzzzzzz

How long do bees live?

Queen bees die in the autumn after 6 or 7 years. Princess and worker bees **hibernate** during winter. The worker bees will die next summer, after the new workers have **hatched**.

Worker bees push the **drones** out of the nest in the autumn and stop them coming back in. The drones die because they have no food to eat.

What do honeybees do?

Some eggs **hatch** into princess bees. When there are too many bees in a nest the old queen takes a **swarm** to find a new nest. A princess becomes the new queen.

Gardeners like worker bees because they take **pollen** from flower to flower and this makes new seeds and new flowers. Many people like to eat the honey that bees make.

How are bees special?

Bees have long hairs on their back legs which work like baskets. They put **pollen** from flowers into the baskets. Their legs look like yellow balloons!

Bees do a special dance to show other bees where there are lots of flowers. Sometimes in the dance, they make a shape like the number 8.

Thinking about bees

Why are bees so busy?

What do worker bees have to do every day?

Would you like to be a **drone**?

This person is collecting honeycombs from the beehive. Why do you think beekeepers wear gloves and a veil? Why do they puff smoke at the bees?

Bug map

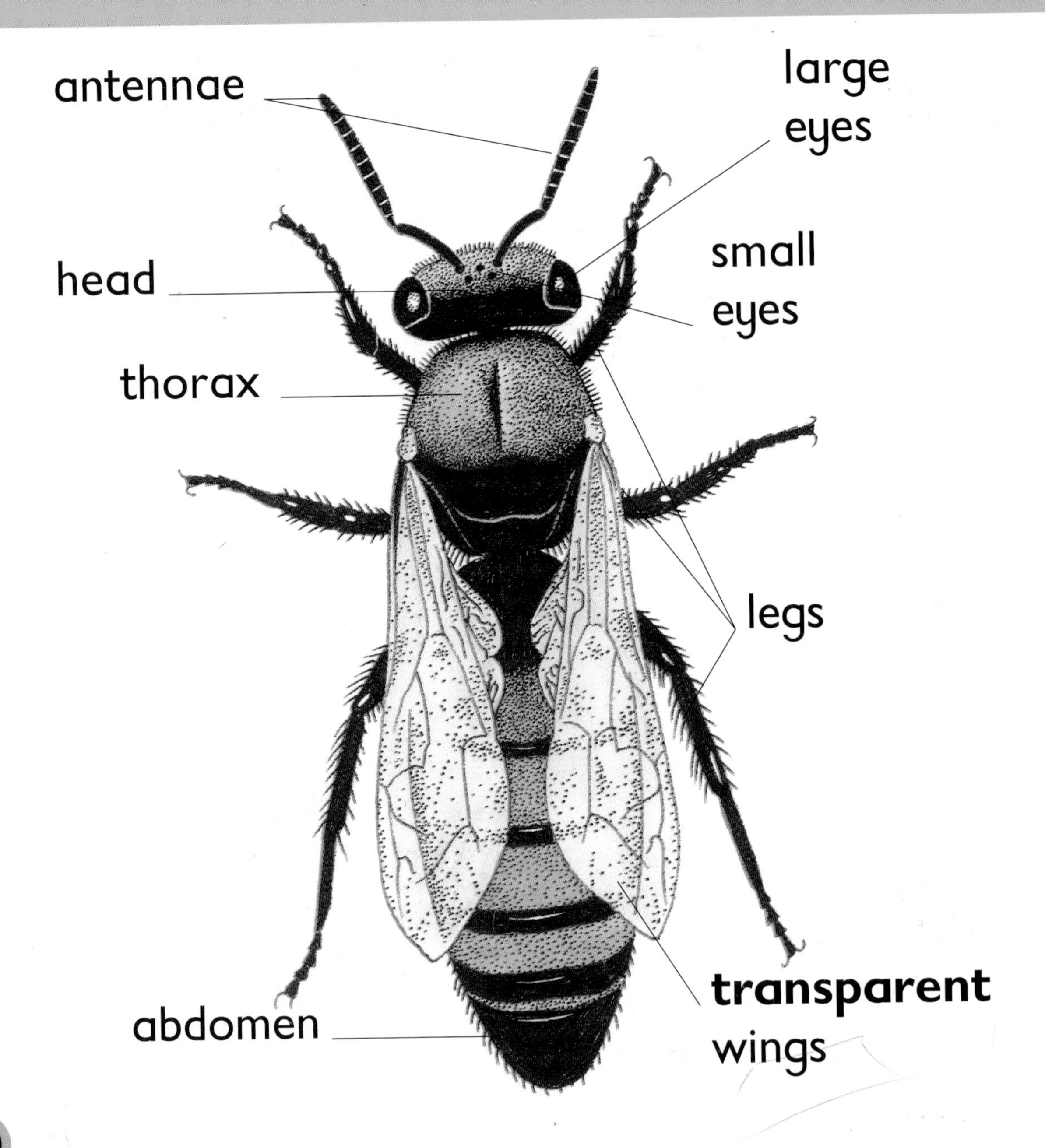
antennae
large
eyes
small
eyes
head
thorax
legs
abdomen
transparent
wings

Glossary

drone a male bee

feelers two long narrow tubes that stick out from the head of an insect. They may be used to feel, smell or even hear.

hatch to come out of an egg pupa

hibernate a special very long sleep that some creatures have during the winter

hollow a hollow tree is usually a dead tree and the trunk is empty inside

insect a small creature with six legs

larva (more than one = larvae) the grub that hatches from the egg

mate male and female bees mate to make baby bees

nectar a sweet juice inside flowers

pollen a golden dust inside flowers

pupa (more than one = pupae) older larva. The adult bees grow inside it.

sting hurting an animal or insect by pricking it with a part of the body that is like a pin

swarm hundreds of bees all flying together to find a new nest

transparent something we can see through clearly

Index